EVERYDAY

Prayers

JOURNAL

Spiritual Refreshment for Women

EVERYDAY

Prayers

JOURNAL

Spiritual Refreshment for Women

BARBOUR
PUBLISHING

ISBN 978-1-60260-621-0

Cover design by Kirk DouPonce, dogeareddesign.com

Published by Barbour Publishing, Inc., P.O. Box 719, Uhrichsville, Ohio 44683, www.barbourbooks.com

Our mission is to publish and distribute inspirational products offering exceptional value and biblical encouragement to the masses.

Member of the
Evangelical Christian
Publishers Association

Printed in the United States of America.

Contents

Introduction

Let us therefore come boldly unto the throne of grace,
that we may obtain mercy, and find grace to help in time of need.

HEBREWS 4:16

What an amazing invitation! We are welcome—any time—to bring any petition before the King of the universe. Not only that, we are also admonished to "come before his presence with thanksgiving" (Psalm 95:2) and "singing" (Psalm 100:2). The all-powerful God we serve is interested in each one of us, and He truly wants to hear what we have to say. That's genuine love!

The words of these prayers are intended to challenge you as you develop a more intimate relationship with your heavenly Father—a relationship He is greatly anticipating.

Anger

If you do not wish to be prone to anger, do not feed the habit;
give it nothing which may tend to its increase.

EPICTETUS

Controlled Anger

I can't take it, Father. It sometimes seems like others deliberately do things to upset me. Maybe it's just how they are with everyone, but I have trouble not retaliating. I try so hard to be like You, but it's a struggle. Please help me control my anger; help me not to be so sensitive.

I Can Do All things thROugH CHRIST wHo StRENGthens mE. I AM A DyNamic Black LaDy. I am StRoNG, Beautiful, SmaRT & Will BE Successful as loNG as I Stay focus & pRayful.

I am 49 yEaRs of aGE. I HavE & WILL coNtinue to Beat any IllNESS oR DiseasE. I am DiseasE-FREE!

I will GET to my WEIGHT-Goal of 155 by the END of DEc. 2014.

StaRting ToDay, DEc. 4th, I will Eat only Two-full meals-a-day. VERy Small SNacks & PleNty of wateR, GReEN-Tea.

lemon w/ warm water.
30-minutes of exercise.
Very moderate Alcohol, if any. Only
on a weekend. I pray for alcohol to
be deleted from my life-style completely.
Today, I am 177.0. I am thankful
to be alive and have my weight, but,
I want to be healthy. I will be healthy!

OK, So I fell off of the band
wagon for a few months!! But I
am still blessed!! Today is a
New Day of Achieving my goals. I
bought some walking sneakers this week.
Starting my journey.

A Waste of Time

I did it again, Lord. I ruined an entire evening because of something incredibly ridiculous.
I didn't sleep well because I was still fuming. My anger is always such a waste of time and energy.
Forgive me, Father. Give me strength to control my temper, and don't let me ruin any more
evenings for myself or for others.

The Right Time and Place

One of the most interesting stories in Your Word is about the time You cleansed the temple. It has taught me that there is a time and place for anger. Sin is always something that should invoke fury. Just help me to direct my anger at the sin and not the sinner.

Calorie Types

Your weight × 8 + 200 = Calorie Type

1500 or below = Low
1500 - 1800 = Medium
1800 - Above = High

Chris Powell
"Extreme Transformation"
Lose Weight in 21-days

Mary Helen Bowers (Balland teachers)
~~Ballet Beautiful~~
on Dr. Oz

Roll-up w/ a twist
→ 12 reps (3 sets) daily
Works core

Reacting Angrily

Father, You know the emotional roller coaster I've been riding. I want to be happy for my friends when they rejoice, but the pain in my heart is so raw. It seems like my loved ones are flaunting their joy, and I can't help but react angrily. I know this hurts them and isn't pleasing to You. Please help me through this struggle.

Anger Hurts

I was just trying to help. I knew from personal experience that he was about to make a mistake. I tried to be gentle and loving, but he became so angry, telling me it was none of my business. Now he won't even speak to me, and that hurts. Please heal the breach, Father.

_____

_____

_____

_____

_____

_____

_____

_____

_____

_____

_____

_____

_____

Children

We can't form our children on our own concepts;
we must take them and love them as God gives them to us.

JOHANN WOLFGANG VON GOETHE

Reality Parenting

From the time I was a child, one of my greatest dreams was to be a mother. I did pretty well when I pretended with my dolls, but reality is a lot different. Now that I have children, I'm not always so sure of myself. Please, God, give me wisdom and courage to be a good parent.

Comic Relief

Children can sometimes be so comical, Lord. They say the funniest things or make the silliest faces. Sometimes all I need to do on a tough day is watch them. They'll do something so hilarious that I can't help but laugh. I feel better right away. Children are a wonderful gift.

_____

_____

_____

_____

_____

_____

_____

_____

_____

_____

_____

_____

_____

_____

_____

_____

_____

_____

_____

_____

_____

_____

_____

_____

_____

_____

_____

_____

_____

_____

_____

Children's Games

Lord, my children love it when I play with them, and sometimes my participation in their activities contributes significantly to their development. But to be honest, I'm not very good at their games. I'm often distracted by other things I need to do. Please don't let me lose sight of the truth—that playing with my children is an important accomplishment.

God's Truths

There's so much I need to teach my children about You, Lord. Throughout their lives there will be so many questions. They will face people and situations that will cause them to doubt You. Give me opportunities to instill Your Word so that when doubts come, they'll stand strong.

_____

_____

_____

_____

_____

_____

_____

_____

_____

_____

_____

_____

_____

_____

_____

_____

_____

_____

_____

_____

_____

_____

_____

_____

_____

_____

_____

_____

_____

_____

_____

_____

A Prayer for My Children

Just the other day someone reminded me of how important it is to pray for my children. So here
I am, Lord. Please protect my kids. Work in their lives, so that they will want to serve You with
body, mind, and soul. Provide those things that they need, and fill them with contentment
as they bask in the warmth of Your love.

Church

Not until I went into the churches of America and heard her pulpits flame
with righteousness did I understand the secret of her genius and power.

ALEXIS DE TOCQUEVILLE

My Church Family

My church is special to me in so many ways, Lord. I am so thankful that You have placed me
among such a wonderful group of believers who encourage me and pray for me. Allow me to be
a blessing to them, as well, and help me to never forget how important they are in my life.

_____

_____

_____

_____

_____

_____

_____

_____

_____

_____

_____

_____

_____

_____

_____

_____

_____

_____

_____

_____

_____

_____

_____

_____

_____

_____

_____

_____

_____

_____

Preaching the Truth

Thank You for my pastor, dear God. He loves You; and he loves those to whom he ministers. Knowing that his desire is to present the truths of the Bible is a great comfort in a world that is full of false teachings. Bless my pastor as he continues to preach Your Word.

Church Decisions

There are many decisions being made on issues concerning our church, Father. They aren't easy decisions to make, and everyone has a different opinion on what the outcome should be. Please give us direction and unity. Work in our midst so that we might bring others into Your kingdom.

_____

_____

_____

_____

_____

_____

_____

_____

_____

_____

_____

_____

_____

_____

_____

_____

_____

_____

_____

_____

_____

_____

_____

_____

_____

_____

_____

_____

_____

_____

_____

_____

_____

_____

Precious People

There are many precious people who offer their time and talents for You, Lord Jesus. I just want to thank You for each one. I appreciate those who make a public contribution as well as those who work behind the scenes. They mean more to me than I can say.

The Pastor's Family

I ask You, Lord, to be with my pastor's family. He puts in many long hours serving You; and although he makes a point to spend time with his wife and children, they still have to make some sacrifices. Bless each one of them as they work to bring Your love to our church and community.

_____

_____

_____

_____

_____

_____

_____

_____

_____

_____

_____

_____

_____

_____

_____

_____

_____

_____

_____

_____

_____

_____

_____

_____

_____

_____

_____

_____

Community

The life I touch for good or ill will touch another life, and that in turn, another,
until who knows where the trembling stops or in what far place my touch will be felt.

FREDERICK BUECHNER

God-Honoring Activities

There are many ways to be involved in my community, Father, and I ask You to show me what to do.
I want to choose the activities that will help others and that will bring glory to You. Help me to
weigh the possibilities carefully and to make the best decisions. Thank You for these opportunities to honor You.

A Witness in My Community

Lord, there are so many people in my community who either don't care about You or who think they will please You by their own merit; but several of them don't truly know You. I ask You to open doors so I may witness to them. My prayer is that many will come to You.

_____

_____

_____

_____

_____

_____

_____

_____

_____

_____

_____

_____

_____

_____

_____

_____

_____

_____

_____

_____

_____

_____

_____

_____

_____

_____

_____

_____

_____

_____

_____

_____

_____

_____

_____

Offering Alternatives

I've noticed many disturbing events in my community, Lord—activities that in no way glorify You.
I don't become involved, but some Christians do, either out of peer pressure or simply because they
don't know it's wrong. Open their eyes. Help us band together to offer Your light in the darkness.

Newcomers

We live in a close-knit community, Lord. In some ways it's nice because we all stick together. At the same time, it can be really hard for newcomers. Some of us try to welcome them, but they often move away before long. Help us, Father, to be more open to new residents in our town.

_____

_____

_____

_____

_____

_____

_____

_____

_____

_____

_____

_____

_____

_____

_____

_____

_____

_____

_____

_____

_____

_____

_____

_____

_____

_____

_____

_____

_____

_____

_____

_____

_____

A Christian Community

I'm thankful for the Christians in my town, dear God. It is such a blessing to fellowship with them. Recently we've started a Bible study that is mostly intended to be an outreach program. Please let it be successful for Your sake.

Contentment

I'm Content

It's a fast-paced world where everyone wants to get ahead, Father. Sometimes contentment is frowned upon. Some folks think of it as laziness or lack of motivation. But I know that if I am in the center of Your will, I'll be content. That's the only true contentment there is.

_____

_____

_____

_____

_____

_____

_____

_____

_____

_____

_____

_____

_____

_____

_____

_____

_____

_____

_____

_____

_____

_____

_____

_____

_____

_____

_____

_____

_____

_____

Consider the Cat

It doesn't take much to please a kitten, does it, Lord? Put him on your lap, rub his head, and listen to him purr. What contentment! I wish I were like that, but it seems the more I gain, the more I strive for. There's not much contentment in that. Let me learn from the cat to be satisfied no matter what!

"Poor Me"

Sometimes my attitude is so "poor me" that I even get sick, Father. I keep thinking that if only I could have this or that, life would be easier. I know I'm missing out on a truly abundant life by whining so much, and I ask You to forgive me. Fill me with contentment.

_____

_____

_____

_____

_____

_____

_____

_____

_____

_____

_____

_____

_____

_____

_____

_____

_____

_____

_____

_____

_____

_____

_____

_____

_____

_____

_____

_____

_____

Labor and Contentment

I am exhausted, Lord, but I don't think I've ever felt better! There's nothing quite like a hard day's work to bring a tremendous amount of satisfaction. And I'm really anticipating the good night's sleep ahead because I know I pleased You with my effort today.

"I Will Never Leave Thee"

You've promised to walk with me all the way and provide all that I need, dear God, and I'm rejoicing in that guarantee. What more do I need? It doesn't matter that the world presents shiny trinkets. Their luster dims in the brilliance of the blessings and contentment that You give.

_____

_____

_____

_____

_____

_____

_____

_____

_____

_____

_____

_____

_____

_____

_____

_____

_____

_____

_____

_____

_____

_____

_____

_____

_____

_____

_____

_____

Discouragement

Permanence, perseverance, and persistence in spite of all obstacles,
discouragements, and impossibilities: It is this, that in all things
distinguishes the strong soul from the weak.

THOMAS CARLYLE

Change of Plans

I feel like crying, Father. We planned to leave for vacation next week, but today my husband was a victim of downsizing. Vacation is now out of the question. He has to find a new job, or we won't be able to pay our bills. Help me to remember that all things work together for good to those who love You.

Drenched Spirits

I was staying on top of my duties for once, Lord. But then the dryer quit working, and I still had piles of laundry to finish. It was fun hanging the clothes out to dry and pretending I was a pioneer—until the rains came. The clothes were drenched, and so were my spirits. I wanted to give up. Please remind me that You are with me through the storms.

Don't Quit

Lord, I don't want to be a quitter; but I've tried so hard to be like You, and I keep messing up.

I know You said that with You all things are possible, and I need to be reminded of that daily.

Don't let me give up. Help me to remember that You aren't finished with me yet.

Count It All as Joy

It's hard to see discouragement as a blessing, Lord. But You said we should count it as joy. The trials will increase my patience and mold me into a more mature believer. When I look at it that way, it's much easier to thank You for the difficult times.

_____

_____

_____

_____

_____

_____

_____

_____

_____

_____

_____

_____

_____

_____

_____

_____

_____

_____

Encouraging Others

You gave me an amazing opportunity today, Father, and it's all a result of a discouraging situation. You helped me as I struggled through the problem, and because of that I was able to encourage someone else who faced a similar difficulty. You really are an awesome God!

Family

*The happiest moments of my life have been the few which
I have passed at home in the bosom of my family.*

THOMAS JEFFERSON

Family Blessings

Among Your many blessings, my family ranks near the top. They share my joys and help bear my burdens. Dear Jesus, I know that You selected each of my relatives to be a part of my life in a special way, and I thank You for each of them. May I bring happiness to them in some way, too!

_____

_____

_____

_____

_____

_____

_____

_____

_____

_____

_____

_____

_____

_____

_____

_____

_____

_____

_____

_____

_____

_____

_____

_____

_____

_____

_____

_____

Godly Parents

Dear Lord, I got my first glimpse of You through the lives of my parents. What a blessing to have two such godly people as an intimate part of my childhood and early adult years. Thank You that they cared enough to instill godly principles in me and loved me enough to introduce me to You.

Family Reunions

We had a family reunion the other day, and I was surprised at how much our family has grown. I used to never really enjoy these gatherings, but this time was different. It was a reminder of the great blessing You've bestowed on me. I realized, also, the opportunity I had to present a testimony of Your love to those who'd never heard. I guess reunions aren't so bad after all.

_____

_____

_____

_____

_____

_____

_____

_____

_____

_____

_____

_____

_____

_____

_____

_____

_____

Facing Differences

Lord, as large as my family is, there are bound to be some members whose life views are significantly different than mine. At times this gets annoying, particularly when they attempt to force their outlook on me. Give me the strength to stand for what I know to be true, and help me to love my family despite our differences.

God's Family

As much as I love my family, I am infinitely more grateful to be part of Your family. To have other believers laugh and cry with me is a beautiful picture of Your love. To be able to pray with them, knowing You are in our midst, is great joy. Thank You for making me Your child.

_____

_____

_____

_____

_____

_____

_____

_____

_____

_____

_____

_____

_____

_____

_____

_____

_____

_____

_____

_____

_____

_____

_____

_____

Fear

Inaction breeds doubt and fear. Action breeds confidence and courage.
If you want to conquer fear, do not sit home and think about it.
Go out and get busy.

DALE CARNEGIE

Peace in the Midst of Terror

Lord, when I think about the world in which I'm raising my children, I tremble. Crime, hatred, terrorism—they're everywhere, and they scare me. I know I should remember that You are in control, and I try, but sometimes I get too caught up in what's happening. Please forgive me, and give me peace.

Fear of the Unknown

I have to laugh when I consider the silly childhood fears I had—mostly fears of the unknown. But when I consider the truth, even now my fears are mostly still of the unknown. It's not so silly now, though, because I should be trusting You instead of worrying. Please help my thoughts to be on You.

_____

_____

_____

_____

_____

_____

_____

_____

_____

_____

_____

_____

_____

_____

_____

_____

_____

_____

_____

_____

_____

_____

_____

_____

_____

_____

_____

_____

_____

_____

_____

_____

_____

_____

Wise Fear

"The fear of the LORD is the beginning of wisdom" (Psalm 111:10). Sometimes this passage from Your Word seems almost contradictory, Lord. But there is healthy fear, and then there's crippling fear. I know this passage means that my respect of You is so deep that I abhor sin. Please help me to have this wise fear.

The Color Yellow

One of the cutest songs I know is about a child peering into a box of crayons and comparing the colors to the Christian life. Yellow represents the cowardly believer—one who is afraid to share Christ's love with others. Please don't let me be yellow. Let me be courageous for You!

_____

_____

_____

_____

_____

_____

_____

_____

_____

_____

_____

_____

_____

_____

_____

_____

_____

Afraid to Surrender

Why are people afraid to surrender their lives to You, Lord? I know some are fearful that You will ask something of them that they can't bear. Can't they understand that You'll strengthen them through every task? Don't they realize the joy they're missing? God, break down the barriers that hinder Your work.

Finances

The real measure of our wealth is how much we'd be worth
if we lost everything.

J. H. JOWETT

Managing Money

It's funny, Lord. It seems like I always wish I had more money, but dealing with it can sometimes be a pain. Keeping it organized, making sure my bills are paid—at times it's overwhelming. Please give me a clear mind and wisdom to handle my financial responsibilities according to Your will.

_____

_____

_____

_____

_____

_____

_____

_____

_____

_____

_____

_____

_____

_____

_____

_____

_____

_____

_____

_____

_____

_____

_____

_____

_____

_____

My Rich Father

Sometimes I find myself worrying about my financial situation. I have a tendency to forget that my Father owns the cattle on a thousand hills—and everything else, too. I know You'll take care of me. Although I might not fully understand wealth in this life, I have amazing riches to anticipate. What a thrill that is!

Healthy Attitudes

So often, Lord, I see relationships crumbling, and much of the time a money issue is what starts the process. Some people are careless or dishonest in their spending; others just want too much. As a result there is a lot of bitterness and hatred. Please help me to have a proper outlook when money is involved.

_____

_____

_____

_____

_____

_____

_____

_____

_____

_____

_____

_____

_____

_____

_____

_____

_____

_____

_____

_____

_____

_____

_____

_____

_____

_____

_____

_____

_____

The Widow's Mites

Lately there have been times when it's been a little hard to tithe. We have trouble paying our bills, so we do without things. The worst thing, though, is thinking about how little our meager contribution actually benefits. Lord, I've been trying to remember the widow's mites, and that does help. Let me take courage from her example.

Extras

Dear God, I am so thankful that You have provided for me. Sometimes that blessing even goes above and beyond my needs. I now ask for wisdom in handling these gifts. My desire is to glorify You and to make sure that I'm not controlled by money. Please help me use it in a way that honors You.

_____

_____

_____

_____

_____

_____

_____

_____

_____

_____

_____

_____

Forgiveness

Forgiveness needs to be accepted, as well as offered, before it is complete.
C. S. Lewis

Opportunities to Forgive

Growing up with ornery siblings, I had plenty of chances to practice forgiveness. I guess that's good because I still have opportunities to forgive. Sometimes it isn't easy, but it feels so much better to let go of the hurt than to hold a grudge. Thank You for giving me these occasions.

Christ Understands

Lord, You've been through things that I will never experience, so You understand how hard it is to forgive. Even though You've experienced the worst insult, You never put me down for thinking that the wrong done to me is unbearable. Instead, You just give me strength to do what is necessary. How can I thank You?

_____

_____

_____

_____

_____

_____

_____

_____

_____

_____

_____

_____

_____

_____

_____

_____

_____

_____

_____

A Friend's Forgiveness

I can't believe it, Father. I really messed up this time, and my friend still forgave me. I didn't really expect her to ever want to speak to me again, but she hugged me and told me we'd just start again. That felt so wonderful! Thank You for friends who forgive.

Natural Consequences

Dear Lord, I know You've forgiven me for that horrible wrong. I thought when I repented that would take care of things, but I'm learning that the natural consequences still hurt. I know they won't disappear, but I pray that You will use them in a positive way—perhaps to keep others from making the same mistake.

_____

_____

_____

_____

_____

_____

_____

_____

_____

_____

_____

_____

_____

_____

_____

_____

_____

_____

_____

_____

_____

_____

_____

_____

_____

_____

_____

_____

_____

_____

_____

_____

_____

Seventy Times Seven

Seventy times seven. Wow! That's an enormous amount of forgiveness, Lord. Looking at it from one perspective, it seems outrageous; but from the other side of the spectrum, I hope someone would do it for me. That's one of the nicest things about forgiveness in the human realm—it's "give and receive."

Friends

Finding Friends

Father, choosing friends isn't always easy. I want to find individuals who share my values and my love for You. There just doesn't seem to be an abundance of people around who care about You. Please lead me to the places where I'll be able to find companions who will glorify You.

_____

_____

_____

_____

_____

_____

_____

_____

_____

_____

_____

_____

_____

_____

_____

_____

_____

_____

_____

_____

_____

_____

_____

_____

_____

_____

_____

_____

_____

_____

_____

_____

Lord, Carry My Friend

My friend is hurting, dear Jesus. She's had so many struggles in her life lately, and she feels like she's about to hit rock bottom. I've tried to be there for her, but right now she needs You in a special way. Please let her know that You want to carry her through this trial. Help her to trust You.

My Best Friend

I think my best friend is a lot like You, Lord. She offers me spiritual encouragement; she's there for me in the happy times and the sad; and she'd do anything for me. How could I not love her? People of her nature are like precious pearls. I'm so blessed to have her in my life!

_____

_____

_____

_____

_____

_____

_____

_____

_____

_____

_____

_____

_____

_____

_____

_____

David and Jonathan

I've been reading about Jonathan and David, Father. What an incredible pair of friends. Jonathan's willingness to take risks on David's behalf is unbelievable, especially considering that he knew David would be king in his place. Lord, that's the kind of friend I want to be.

Unequally Yoked

I guess I've always wanted to give people the benefit of the doubt, but I haven't always been careful enough. I've ended up becoming too close to people who disregard You, and sometimes their influence on me has been too great. Father, please help me be friendly but not intimate with unbelievers.

_____

_____

_____

_____

_____

_____

_____

_____

_____

_____

_____

_____

_____

_____

_____

_____

_____

_____

_____

_____

_____

_____

_____

_____

_____

_____

Goals

I know the price of success: dedication, hard work,
and an unremitting devotion to the things you want to see happen.

FRANK LLOYD WRIGHT

Reached Goals

Sometimes I get a little discouraged, Jesus. I feel like I've reached all the goals I've set for myself
and that there's nothing for me to achieve that would bring any excitement. Please give me a new
outlook. Give me wisdom as I set new goals, and help me to give You the glory when I succeed.

To-Do Lists

I didn't really think my goals were far-fetched. My to-do list only had three major tasks, yet I barely made it through two. It seems I've worked all day and accomplished nothing. I feel disgusted with myself, but tomorrow's another day, Lord. Give me the right attitude as I begin again.

_____

_____

_____

_____

_____

_____

_____

_____

_____

_____

_____

_____

_____

_____

_____

_____

_____

_____

_____

_____

_____

_____

_____

_____

_____

_____

_____

_____

_____

_____

_____

_____

_____

_____

Consulting Christ

Lord, often in my daily planning I forget to consult You. Then I wonder why things don't work out the way I think they should. Forgive my arrogant attitude. I know that only as You guide me through the day will I find joy in accomplishments. Show me how to align my goals with Your will.

Blank Stares

Today I'm struggling, Jesus. I have a specific goal that needs to be met, but it requires clarity of mind. The project is spread out before me, but I'm staring at it blankly. I know You want me to work on it, and I need Your guidance. Give me the ability to think and complete the task.

_____

_____

_____

_____

_____

_____

_____

_____

_____

_____

_____

_____

_____

_____

_____

_____

_____

Thank You for Goals

Thank You for goals, Lord. Although they require work, they give me something to look forward to. The effort put forth is exhilarating, and the sense of accomplishment rewarding. You make me a stronger person just by giving me work to do.

Godly Character

The Christian idea has not been tried and found wanting.
It has been found difficult and left untried.

G. K. CHESTERTON

Reality Strikes

Dear God, sometimes godly character sounds so easy to attain when I'm sitting in church, listening to the pastor speak. In my heart I know I want it; in my mind I believe it's possible. Making the ideal become reality is much harder. I need Your strength. Please help me develop godly character.

_____

_____

_____

_____

_____

_____

_____

_____

_____

_____

_____

_____

Godly Examples

I've seen quite a few examples of godly people, and I'm so thankful You've allowed them to cross my path, Father. It's a real encouragement to see other people who are becoming more and more like You. It helps me in my own quest for Christlikeness. Thank You for bringing these individuals into my life.

Special Instructions

Thank You for Your Word, Father. Without it I would be a helpless cause in regard to developing godly character. I'm so glad You preserved these special words that give me specific instruction on how to live. Help me to hide these scriptures in my heart so that I'm able to rely on them throughout my life.

_____

_____

_____

_____

_____

_____

_____

_____

_____

_____

_____

_____

_____

_____

_____

_____

_____

_____

Being Godly on Purpose

Lord, I was recently reminded that godly character doesn't just happen. I have to purpose in my heart to live a life pleasing to You. Only then will I be able to stand strong when peer pressure threatens to undo me. I want to commit daily to obeying You.

Awake to Righteousness

You are far from silent about how You expect me to live, dear God. You've commanded me to be like You, and that includes righteous living. You've explicitly said, "Awake to righteousness, and sin not" (1 Corinthians 15:34). I don't know if the message could be any more plain. I must be righteous!

_____

_____

_____

_____

_____

_____

_____

_____

_____

_____

_____

_____

_____

_____

_____

_____

_____

_____

_____

_____

_____

_____

_____

_____

_____

_____

_____

_____

_____

_____

_____

God's Will

I find that doing God's will leaves me
no time for disputing about His plans.

George MacDonald

The Center of God's Will

Lord, I know that in the center of Your will are peace, joy, and many other rich blessings. I'd like to experience all these things, but the trouble I seem to have is figuring out what Your will is for me. Please help me be attentive when You speak, and give me a heart willing to be used by You.

Specifics in God's Word

Sometimes I get so frustrated, Lord. I've asked what You want from me, but it seems You've remained silent. Then I realize that there are specifics in Your Word that I should automatically be doing. I haven't always been obedient to those, so how can I expect to know more? Forgive me, Father. I want to obey.

_____

_____

_____

_____

_____

_____

_____

_____

_____

_____

_____

_____

_____

_____

_____

_____

_____

_____

The Bigger Picture

There have been some things happening lately that I just don't understand, Lord. I know You see the bigger picture and that all that happens is part of Your plan, but sometimes I need a reminder. Help me focus on the promise that all things work together for good to those who love You.

God's Will for Loved Ones

I've spent a lot of time praying about Your will in my life, Lord, but I have many loved ones who also need to know the work You have for them. Help them to be open to Your leading, and give me grace to accept what You call them to—even if it's not what I had in mind.

_____

_____

_____

_____

_____

_____

_____

_____

_____

_____

_____

_____

_____

_____

_____

_____

_____

_____

_____

_____

God Won't Force It

Your desire is that we seek and do Your will, dear God, but You'll never force us to do it. You've laid unique paths before each of us, and it's because You love us all in a special way. Help us not to envy Your plans for others; let us complete our work with joy.

Grief

If we had no winter, the spring would not be so pleasant; if we did not sometimes taste of adversity, prosperity would not be so welcome.

ANNE BRADSTREET

Deep Sorrow

I know You understand grief better than anyone else, Father, but right now I feel as if no one has traveled this road before. My sorrow is so deep, my pain so intense. It seems I'm all alone. I need You, God. My soul cries out for relief. Please heal my broken heart, and help me smile once more.

_____

_____

_____

_____

_____

_____

_____

_____

_____

_____

_____

_____

_____

_____

_____

_____

_____

_____

Loss of a Pet

My child's dog died this morning, Lord, and he is full of sorrow. Some mock his tears, but his grief is very real to him. I hug him close and offer words of comfort, but that won't bring back his playmate. Please fill the void in his life, and comfort him in Your special way.

God's Comfort

Dear Jesus, my sister is grieving for her son who rejects You. My friend is losing her father to a dreadful illness. My neighbor's marriage is crumbling despite her best efforts to pull it together. They need Your comfort. They, and so many like them. Soothe their heartaches, Father.

_____

_____

_____

_____

_____

_____

_____

_____

_____

_____

_____

_____

_____

_____

_____

_____

_____

_____

_____

_____

_____

_____

_____

_____

_____

_____

_____

_____

_____

_____

_____

_____

Freedom to Grieve

It's so hard to express grief in our society, Jesus, but I'm glad You don't reject us when we do. After all, You grieved, and You showed me how to handle perhaps one of the deepest human emotions. Thank You for letting me come to You when I'm hurting. Thank You for Your love.

Yes, God Loves Me

I've been concentrating so much on my grief, Lord, that I'm afraid my perspective of You has become warped. I wonder why You allow bad things to happen, and sometimes I even question whether or not You really love me. I know the truth is that You are right there with me, wanting me to trust and love You more. Help me keep that in focus.

Happiness

It's not how much we have, but how much
we enjoy, that makes happiness.

CHARLES SPURGEON

Those Happy Times

A lot of times I've heard people say that Christians can be joyful without being happy, and I know that's true. Still, I relish those happy times in life. It feels good to laugh so hard that I'm crying and to smile because I see something cute. Thank You for giving me happy times to enjoy, dear Jesus.

Bearable Burdens

Lord, we sometimes sing a song about being happy because You took our burdens all away. I guess You really just make the burdens more bearable. Still, that's something great to sing about, and it does bring happiness. I'm so glad You're there to lighten the load.

_____

_____

_____

_____

_____

_____

_____

_____

_____

_____

_____

_____

_____

_____

Simple Blessings

Thank You for the many happy times You've given me. So often it's the little things in life—the first robin in the spring, the first homegrown tomato of the season, even a brilliant sunset. These simple blessings evoke the biggest smiles and make me the happiest!

Bad Happiness

I'm embarrassed, Lord, and I need Your cleansing. Someone at church has been giving me trouble for a while. I just discovered that something unfortunate happened to him, and I gloated. I tried to keep my happiness undercover, but it was there, and it shouldn't have been. Please don't let me rejoice at others' misfortune.

The Source of Happiness

I'm glad money isn't required to obtain true happiness, or I wouldn't get much. You meet my needs sufficiently, but the happiness I enjoy when I'm with family or just relaxing with a good book on a lazy afternoon is beyond sufficient. True happiness really can't be bought, can it, Jesus? It all comes from You.

Health

If taking vitamins doesn't keep you healthy enough, try more laughter:
The most wasted of all days is that on which one has not laughed.

NICOLAS-SEBASTIEN CHAMFORT

What's Right?

Sometimes I get pretty confused, Lord. I try to eat right, exercise properly, and get plenty of rest, but all of the "experts" say different things about what I should be doing. It's important that I am a good steward of the body You've given me, so please help me to care for myself the right way.

_____

_____

_____

_____

_____

_____

_____

_____

_____

_____

_____

_____

_____

_____

_____

_____

_____

Enjoying Good Health

I thank You, Father, for giving me good health. There are so many who do not enjoy this blessing. Sometimes I'm tempted to complain about the aches and pains that we all face from time to time, but I really have no reason to. You have been good to me.

Sufficient Grace

I've been facing a physical difficulty lately, and it seems to be getting worse. I've prayed, dear God. Oh, how I've prayed. Sometimes it feels like You are so far away, but I know You are right here next to me, offering Your sufficient grace and strength. Help me to accept this as Your answer.

_____

_____

_____

_____

_____

_____

_____

_____

_____

_____

_____

_____

_____

_____

_____

_____

_____

_____

_____

_____

_____

_____

_____

_____

_____

_____

_____

_____

_____

_____

_____

_____

_____

_____

Sick Children

Dear Lord, all the kids are sick, and I am at my wit's end. They don't understand why they're miserable. All I can do is hold them close and let them know I love them, but sometimes I wonder if it's enough. I ask You to heal them. Please help me be the mother they need.

Christ Still Heals

You brought healing to so many people in the Bible, Jesus. Those were exciting times for those individuals, and it's still a spectacular miracle when You make someone whole today. Thank You for the many times You've touched my sick body or brought relief to my loved ones. Your loving touch produces great joy.

_____

_____

_____

_____

_____

_____

_____

_____

_____

_____

_____

_____

_____

_____

Home

Mid pleasures and palaces, though we may roam,
Be it ever so humble, there's no place like home.

JOHN HOWARD PAYNE

Filled with Love

Lord, let my home be a comforting haven for my family and friends. May it be a place where they can momentarily escape the pressures of this world. Help me to do my best to make it a place where people will know they are loved by me and, more importantly, by You.

Where the Heart Is

I've heard it said that home is where the heart is, and I suppose there's a lot of truth in that. My home is such a special place, and it seems that often when I'm somewhere else, I am longing to be back in that place, surrounded by what is comfortable and familiar. Thank You for that opportunity to return home.

_____

_____

_____

_____

_____

_____

_____

_____

_____

_____

_____

_____

_____

_____

_____

_____

_____

_____

_____

_____

_____

_____

_____

_____

_____

_____

_____

_____

_____

_____

_____

Welcome to My Home

Do You feel welcome in my home, Father? Are You happy to be here, or are You ashamed to call me Your child? I want You to be more important in our daily lives than anything else, and I want to open our home to You to use in any way You choose.

The Real Me

It's not that I mean to be two-faced, Lord, but I guess I'm just more comfortable at home. I'm not as careful about what I say, and often my weaknesses seem exaggerated because I'm not always on guard. That's how I end up hurting those I love the most. Father, please let the "real me" be Christlike at home—and away.

_____

_____

_____

_____

_____

_____

_____

_____

_____

_____

_____

_____

_____

_____

_____

_____

_____

_____

Family Time

Thank You for my home, dear Jesus. I just love to be here. I can't explain the joy that comes from being surrounded by those I love. Whether our home is filled with laughter during game night or shrouded in silent contemplation during family devotions, I can feel Your presence, and I am uplifted.

Humility

God created the world out of nothing, and so long as we are nothing,
He can make something out of us.

MARTIN LUTHER

Unnatural Humility

We're by nature very proud, Jesus. Humility certainly doesn't come easily. But You are humble, and You are the example I am to follow regardless of what comes readily. Teach me to be more like You. Teach me to be a servant.

_____

_____

_____

_____

_____

_____

_____

_____

_____

_____

_____

_____

_____

_____

_____

_____

_____

_____

To Be Like Jesus

Father, I was amazed to see a very attractive, well-dressed lady go out of her way to help an individual of completely opposite description. The dirt and smell didn't seem to bother her, and the heartfelt hug so brightened the other person's countenance. I thought how like You the lady was—how like You I want to be.

Behind the Scenes

There are so many people who desire those high-profile positions, and there's nothing wrong with that; but I want to thank You for those people who are cheerfully willing to take the less-noticeable jobs. Their humble contributions help things run more smoothly, and that's how I want to be—willing to do whatever needs to be done.

_____

_____

_____

_____

_____

_____

_____

_____

_____

_____

_____

_____

_____

_____

_____

_____

_____

Humiliating Lessons

A promotion opportunity came up at work, and I felt like I met the qualifications. I was sure
I would get the job, but an outsider was hired instead. That stung! I guess if I had learned to be
humble in the first place, it might not have hurt so badly. Let me learn from this, Jesus.

Resolving Arguments

I overheard an argument and witnessed a display of true humility, Lord. One individual had a legitimate gripe, yet he backed down from the other person just to resolve the quarrel. He obviously wasn't afraid of the other person; he just wanted the friendship restored. That's how You want us to react, isn't it?

_____

_____

_____

_____

_____

_____

_____

_____

_____

_____

_____

_____

Joy

The joy of the Lord will arm us against the assaults of our spiritual enemies
and put our mouths out of taste for those pleasures
with which the tempter baits his hooks.

MATTHEW HENRY

A New Song

Since You came into my life, dear Jesus, I am filled with a fascinating joy. You've given me a new
song, and I find myself singing it at the most unusual times. Sometimes I receive questioning
looks, but it gives me an opportunity to share with others what You've done in my life. I pray they
seek Your joy, too.

Songs of Joy

I love listening to children singing songs about joy. They're such positive tunes, and I find myself wanting to join in. And why shouldn't I? I'm sure it would please You to hear adults belting out these joyful Sunday school verses with as much conviction as the little ones. After all, You've given us our joy.

_____

_____

_____

_____

_____

_____

_____

_____

_____

_____

_____

_____

_____

_____

_____

_____

J-O-Y

Jesus—others—you. What a simple yet profound definition of joy. And I'm beginning to see just how much this really works. I guess that's because when You are first in my life, everything else is properly prioritized. Although putting others before myself isn't always easy, it feels wonderful when I do it.

Joyful Knowledge

Although the world might not think that my circumstances always warrant a song, I am rejoicing in the knowledge of what lies ahead. I have perfect hope of an eternity with You. I have joy in the belief that You are with me each step of the way. You have put a smile in my heart. Thank You, Lord.

_____

_____

_____

_____

_____

_____

_____

_____

_____

_____

_____

_____

_____

_____

_____

_____

_____

Tidings of Joy

You brought joy to Abraham and Sarah when You said they'd have a son. In a similar way, Mary rejoiced. And the many times You announced, "Thy faith hath saved thee," brought forth smiles. Your Word still has that effect today. Thank You for giving us joy!

Life's Challenges

Many men owe the grandeur of their lives
to their tremendous difficulties.

CHARLES H. SPURGEON

A New Challenge Each Day

Oh, how I enjoy a good challenge, Lord; and each day challenges me anew! Thank You for these opportunities—for each exciting adventure. My desire is that I might face each task in a godly manner and that I might honor You in all I say and do.

_____

_____

_____

_____

_____

_____

_____

_____

_____

_____

_____

_____

_____

_____

_____

_____

_____

_____

_____

_____

_____

_____

_____

_____

_____

_____

_____

_____

_____

Joy in the Challenge

Father, I thought challenges were supposed to be positive motivation, but when I woke up this morning, I'm afraid my outlook wasn't very optimistic. All I could think about were the myriad mundane jobs I had to do. Forgive me. Help me to accept each challenge with joy.

Godly Patience

I have to admit that one of the greatest challenges I face each day is the need for patience. I'm tested regularly on the subject, and too often I fail. Lord, I know I won't win this battle overnight, but with Your help, I'll daily work toward achieving godly patience.

_____

_____

_____

_____

_____

_____

_____

_____

_____

_____

_____

_____

_____

_____

_____

_____

_____

_____

_____

_____

_____

_____

_____

_____

_____

_____

_____

_____

_____

_____

_____

_____

A Definition

Life's challenge—how can I describe it? I might say it is my best-laid plans peppered with interruptions, broken equipment, lack of sleep, and the necessity to complete a task in the allotted amount of time regardless of the circumstances. It sounds rough, and it often seems that way, but with Your help I can endure!

Joshua's Example

Joshua faced a tough challenge, didn't he, Lord? He had to get a rather difficult group of people across a huge river right at flood stage, and that was merely the beginning. But he didn't flinch. He trusted Your promises to be with him, and I can, too. Thank You for reminding me of Joshua's example right when I needed it most.

_____

_____

_____

_____

_____

_____

_____

_____

_____

_____

_____

_____

_____

_____

_____

_____

_____

_____

_____

_____

_____

_____

_____

_____

_____

_____

Loneliness

An infinite God can give all of Himself to each of His children.
He does not distribute Himself that each may have a part,
but to each one He gives all of Himself as fully as if there were no others.

A. W. TOZER

Monday Holidays

I used to love Monday holidays, Lord. The long weekends, the picnics, and family fun—I have great memories. But now it's different. I live too far away to go home. My friends are with their families, and I don't want to intrude. But I'm lonely. Please ease that emptiness, and help me reach out to others in similar situations.

Christ's Loneliness

Lord, how alone You must have been in the garden when the disciples fell asleep. And when God turned His back as You hung on the cross—was there anything to compare to what You felt? Yet You did it willingly. You understand when I'm lonely, and I thank You for being there during those times.

_____

_____

_____

_____

_____

_____

_____

_____

_____

_____

_____

_____

_____

_____

_____

_____

_____

_____

_____

_____

_____

_____

_____

_____

_____

_____

_____

_____

_____

_____

_____

A Lonely World

It can be a lonely world at times—especially when people don't understand why I choose to serve You. I guess it kind of makes me homesick for heaven. I can't wait to be with You forever and to spend time with others who are praising You, too!

Reaching Out

Dear God, I was just noticing all the people around me who really could use a friend. For whatever reason, they're alone and hurting. I need to reach out to them. I ask You to give me opportunities and ideas to let them know I care. Let me make the world a little friendlier for them.

The Right Solution

Father, a friend of mine got tired of being the only "single" around. We tried to ease the loneliness, but she felt that marriage was the only answer. She fell for the first guy who showed interest, and now she's even more miserable. Please give her strength, and help others learn from her mistake.

Love

The best portion of a good man's life,
His little, nameless, unremembered acts, of kindness and of love.

WILLIAM WORDSWORTH

True Love

Love—what a beautiful word! Yet many people are so cynical about it, dear Jesus. I guess that's because there is so much artificial affection in this world, but I'd like for people to see true love—Your love—in my life. Please give me the ability to love as You do.

_____

_____

_____

_____

_____

_____

_____

_____

_____

_____

_____

_____

_____

_____

_____

_____

_____

_____

_____

_____

_____

_____

_____

_____

_____

_____

_____

_____

_____

_____

Loving God

I say I love You, Father, although I'm not sure it goes as deep as it should. I want it to, though.
I want to be so in love with You that it shows in every aspect of my life. Help me to develop the
intimacy with You that I should have.

I Love You

Today my little girl turned her cherubic face toward me and said so sincerely, "I love you." She doesn't fully understand, but she means it as best as she knows how. Just to hear those precious words in her sweet little voice brightened my day, and I thank You for that blessing.

_____

_____

_____

_____

_____

_____

_____

_____

_____

_____

_____

_____

_____

_____

_____

_____

_____

_____

_____

_____

_____

_____

_____

_____

_____

_____

_____

_____

_____

_____

_____

_____

Love and Fear

Looking at it from a human perspective, it doesn't seem like love and fear are remotely connected. Yet we are admonished many times to love and fear You. It's a little hard to comprehend, but when we really consider who You are and what You've done for us, how can we not both fear and love You?

No Excuses

I want to say, "You don't know what that person's like. He's impossible to love!" But You told me to love my enemies. You showed me how to do this by dying for me even when my life was loathsome from sin. I was hideous, unlovable, but You still cared. I have no excuse not to love my enemies.

_____

_____

_____

_____

_____

_____

_____

_____

_____

_____

_____

_____

_____

_____

_____

_____

_____

_____

_____

_____

_____

_____

_____

_____

_____

_____

_____

_____

_____

Missions

The history of missions is the
history of answered prayer.

SAMUEL ZWERNER

—— ◦◦◦ ——

Provision for Missions

In Your Word, You've commanded us to take the gospel to all nations. You've also said that when we're obedient, You'll meet our needs. Please meet the needs of our missionaries, Lord. Provide what they need physically and spiritually, and let many souls be saved as a result.

World Missions and Me

Father, I believe the mission field You have for me is right here at home, but I know You want me to be involved in world missions, as well. Help me to faithfully pray for our missionaries. Give me wisdom as to how You would have me financially support them, and show me any other way I can help them.

_____

_____

_____

_____

_____

_____

_____

_____

_____

_____

_____

_____

_____

_____

_____

_____

_____

_____

_____

_____

_____

_____

_____

_____

_____

_____

_____

_____

_____

_____

_____

In Harm's Way

Dear God, so many missionaries are in harm's way. They face terrorist threats, unsanitary living conditions, and even dangerous animals or illnesses that I can't begin to fathom. Please protect them, Father. They've willingly taken these risks so that others might know Your love. Keep them under Your wing of safety.

Now Entering the Mission Field

There is a sign over the door at church that states, YOU ARE NOW ENTERING THE MISSION FIELD. You called it harvest, Lord, and You want me to do my part in gathering. Lead me to souls who are prepared for the gospel. Let me be alert to opportunities to witness for You.

_____

_____

_____

_____

_____

_____

_____

_____

_____

_____

_____

_____

_____

_____

_____

_____

_____

Those Left Behind

Father, I'd like to take just a moment to pray for the extended families of missionaries. We often forget that as obedient servants take Your gospel abroad, their relatives are left behind. The separation can be difficult. Ease the loneliness. Bless each family member in a special way.

Modesty

Modesty is to merit, what shade is to figures in a picture;
it gives strength and makes it stand out.

JEAN DE LA BRUYERE

An Immodest World

Your Word clearly demands modesty of Your children, God, but to be honest, it's hard in this world. It's difficult to even find apparel that would fit Your definition of modesty, and the attitudes of people are even more indecent. I need Your strength to obey even when it's not easy.

_____

_____

_____

_____

_____

_____

_____

_____

_____

_____

_____

_____

_____

_____

_____

_____

_____

_____

_____

_____

_____

_____

_____

_____

_____

_____

_____

_____

_____

Modest Example

So many people think that modesty is only a clothing issue, but You've shown me that it's so much more. It's an attitude akin to humility, and it's what You want from me. Even in this You set the example for me, Jesus. Help me to follow the pattern You've given me.

My Heavenly Mansion

Enormous homes seem to be what are expected in this "get more" society. Calling someone's home "modest" is almost derogatory, and that's a shame. Help me not to envy those who have more. My home meets my needs and gives me something to look forward to as I anticipate my heavenly mansion.

_____

_____

_____

_____

_____

_____

_____

_____

_____

_____

_____

_____

_____

_____

_____

_____

_____

_____

_____

_____

_____

_____

_____

_____

_____

_____

_____

_____

_____

_____

_____

Praise Be to God

I guess we all like to receive praise from time to time, and in moderation it's probably good for us. But, Father, give me a modest heart about the honor when it does come. Don't let me become puffed with pride. I want to give the glory to You, for without You I am nothing.

Don't Strut Your Stuff

You've allowed me to excel at some things, dear God, and I'm glad to be of use to You. But there have been times I've been a little embarrassed because others want me to flaunt my accomplishments. I know sometimes sharing what I've done will benefit others, but help me to distinguish between helpfulness and bragging.

_____

_____

_____

_____

_____

_____

_____

_____

_____

_____

_____

_____

_____

_____

_____

_____

Neighbors

Intercessory prayer might be defined
as loving our neighbor on our knees.

CHARLES BRENT

The Folks Next Door

I didn't have many neighbors growing up, and I'd heard a lot of horror stories about neighbors in general. When I moved into my own home, I was more than a little leery about the folks next door. It didn't take long to realize what a blessing they are. I only pray that I'll be a good neighbor in return.

That Important First Step

Lord, my neighbors are some of the most rude and inconsiderate people I've ever known. It's hard not to complain about them, but I don't have a right to. They aren't Christians, and I've never witnessed to them. Why would they act differently? Forgive me, Father. I will take them Your Word. Please open their hearts.

_____

_____

_____

_____

_____

_____

_____

_____

_____

_____

_____

_____

_____

_____

_____

_____

_____

_____

_____

_____

_____

_____

_____

_____

_____

_____

_____

_____

_____

Who Is My Neighbor?

One young man asked You who his neighbor was, and You told him the story of the good Samaritan. I've always admired the Samaritan, but I sometimes find I'm more like the priest or Levite, finding reasons not to help others. How this must hurt You! Cleanse me, Lord. Mold me into a good neighbor.

Weekday Christians

There's a lot of importance to be placed on making sure we're godly, not only on Sunday but throughout the week. After all, that's mostly when our neighbors see us. I'm so grateful for godly neighbors who live their faith on a daily basis, Lord. Their influence on me is profound.

_____

_____

_____

_____

_____

_____

_____

_____

_____

_____

_____

_____

_____

_____

_____

_____

_____

_____

_____

_____

_____

_____

_____

_____

_____

_____

_____

_____

_____

_____

_____

_____

Neighborly Influence

I'm a little concerned about the effect some of my neighbors might be having upon my children, Lord. I've tried to bring them up according to Your Word, but peer pressure can be quite strong. Please help them to be faithful and to stay on the right path.

Our Country and Leaders

Providence has given to our people the choice of their rulers, and it is the duty,
as well as the privilege and interest of our Christian nation,
to select and prefer Christians for their rulers.

JOHN JAY

Our Freedom

It brings tears to my eyes just to hear "The Star-Spangled Banner," and I get choked up when I see veterans being honored. I know it's because of the sacrifices made by others that I have freedom to worship You as I choose. Thank You for my country. May I never take these liberties for granted.

_____

_____

_____

_____

_____

_____

_____

_____

_____

_____

_____

_____

_____

_____

_____

_____

_____

_____

_____

_____

_____

_____

_____

_____

_____

_____

_____

One Nation Under God

Dear God, I am so weary of the bickering in our nation. It disturbs me to see people attempting to remove You from schools, courtrooms, and anywhere else they think of. They distort history and deny that this nation was founded with You as her leader. Heal us, Lord. Help us return to You!

Righteous Leaders

You've said that having righteous leaders results in rejoicing among the people, and You've given us the opportunity to choose our leaders. With this privilege, You've given us the responsibility of electing godly people. Father, give us wisdom to recognize these individuals and to put them into office.

_____

_____

_____

_____

_____

_____

_____

_____

_____

_____

_____

_____

_____

_____

_____

_____

Righteousness Exalteth a Nation

I love the Proverbs, Lord, and one of my favorites says, "Righteousness exalteth a nation" (Proverbs 14:34). For many years our country has been powerful among her peers, and it's because You were part of the lives of the people. We've begun to abandon You, though. Please forgive us, and restore us to a right relationship with You.

On Behalf of Our Soldiers

There is a very special group of Americans whom I'd like to bring before You, Father. They are our servicemen and -women. So many of them are in harm's way, Lord. They need Your protection in a way I cannot even comprehend. Please put a hedge around them. Bring them safely home.

_____

_____

_____

_____

_____

_____

_____

_____

_____

_____

_____

_____

Peace

A great many people are trying to make peace, but that has already been done.
God has not left it for us to do; all we have to do is enter into it.

D. L. MOODY

Gentle Peace

Thank You, Lord, for this opportunity to bask in the peace that You offer. As I sit here in the woods, listening to the creek gently bubbling over the stones, I am reminded how Your presence in my life soothes even in the midst of chaos. I'm glad I have Your peace!

The Gift of Peace

Father, as I look around, I see so much turmoil. My heart breaks as I watch the trials people attempt to face without You in their lives. They don't realize the perfect peace that You want to give them, and many of them don't want to hear about it. Speak to their hearts. Help them accept Your gift.

_____

_____

_____

_____

_____

_____

_____

_____

_____

_____

_____

_____

_____

_____

_____

_____

_____

Peaceful Rest

How beautiful to watch a sleeping child! With his arm wrapped gently around his teddy bear and his thumb in his mouth, he embodies peacefulness. As I watch him, I am reminded that You've promised peaceful rest to those in Your care. Oh, how I thank You for this!

Butter-Tub Ships

Last week was pretty hectic, dear Jesus, but I was reminded that You hadn't forgotten me. My daughter came home with a butter tub that had been converted into a ship. It was accompanied by a picture of You calming the storm. Across the top were emblazoned the words, PEACE BE STILL.

_____

_____

_____

_____

_____

_____

_____

_____

_____

_____

_____

_____

_____

_____

_____

_____

_____

_____

_____

_____

_____

_____

_____

_____

_____

_____

_____

_____

_____

At Peace with Others

There are a lot of people with whom I must get along. We come from a variety of backgrounds, and we don't always agree on everything. I've found, however, that peaceful disagreement makes for better relationships, so help me to do my part to live peaceably with others.

Prayers of Praise

Praise God, from whom all blessings flow; Praise Him, all creatures here below;
Praise Him above, ye heav'nly host; Praise Father, Son, and Holy Ghost.

THOMAS KEN, "DOXOLOGY"

Evening Rainbows

When I first caught a glimpse of that rainbow, I was thrilled. When I really stopped to look at its brilliance, I was awed. Only You could have painted something so glorious across the expanse of the evening sky. Thank You for the beauty of Your promises.

_____

_____

_____

_____

_____

_____

_____

_____

_____

_____

_____

_____

_____

_____

_____

_____

_____

All Creation Speaks

We've traveled through several states recently and seen many scenic pictures. Golden fields, purple mountains, sparkling lakes. . . How could anyone believe that something so amazing just happened? Your awesome creation speaks the truth, and to You belongs all the glory!

Matchless Grace

The song talks of praising You for Your matchless grace, and how could I go through a single day without doing so? I don't understand why You love and forgive me, but I wish to offer my sincerest thanks for these bountiful gifts. You are a wonderful Savior!

For Each New Day

Every day there is something for which I can offer You praise, dear God! To begin with, we have the promise of a fresh start—a new opportunity to serve You. Throughout the day You show Your majesty in a multitude of ways. You are an awesome God!

Sacrifice of Praise

Lord, may the life I live be a continual sacrifice of praise to You. You, who have done so much for me, ask only that I give my life wholly to You. How can I refuse? Let what others see in me be cause for them to glorify You, too.

_____

_____

_____

_____

_____

_____

_____

_____

_____

_____

_____

_____

_____

Prayers of Thanks

Best of all is it to preserve everything in a pure, still heart; and let
there be for every pulse a thanksgiving, and for every breath a song.

KONRAD VON GESNER

New Compassions

I really didn't want to get up this morning, Father. My blankets seemed like good protection from
the cares of the day. But when I saw the glorious sunrise and heard the cheerful, singing birds,
I was reminded that Your compassions are new every morning. I knew everything would be fine.
Thank You for Your faithfulness.

God's in Control

Thank You, Lord, that You have a perfect plan for my life. I know I don't always understand it, but You know what's best, and everything that happens is for a reason—that You might be glorified. I'm so glad that You are in control and that I need not worry.

_____

_____

_____

_____

_____

_____

_____

_____

_____

_____

_____

_____

_____

_____

_____

_____

_____

_____

_____

_____

_____

_____

_____

_____

_____

_____

_____

_____

_____

Summer Rains

That refreshing rain! Oh, how badly we needed it. The fields were parched and the rivers drying. Just when we thought we could take no more of the heat, You sent the cool, cleansing rains. Now the garden's growing, the streams are flowing, and our hearts are offering thanks!

O Give Thanks unto the Lord

Father, I was working on a series of lessons for the children's Sunday school, and I felt led to concentrate on the verse that says, "O give thanks unto the Lord" (Psalm 136:1). I realized how many things we have to be thankful for and how many lessons in Your Word back this up. You are indeed worthy of our thanks!

_____

_____

_____

_____

_____

_____

_____

_____

_____

_____

_____

_____

_____

_____

_____

_____

_____

_____

_____

_____

_____

_____

_____

_____

_____

_____

_____

_____

_____

_____

Thank You for the Lightning Bugs

I am convinced, Father, that one reason You bring children across our paths is to teach us important lessons. It wasn't long ago that I heard a small child thanking You for many things. "And thank You for the lightning bugs," he said. What a simple reminder that there's nothing too insignificant for which to offer thanks.

Purity

The name of Jesus. . .awakened similar emotions in the hearts of all the converts
and called immediately into action every feeling of moral loveliness
and every desire of dutiful obedience, which constitute Christian purity.

JOHN STRACHAN

Think on Pure Things

There's just not much in today's society that encourages purity, but Your Word certainly demonstrates the importance of focusing our attention upon things that are pure. From experience, I have learned that life is more satisfying when it's geared toward pleasing You rather than the flesh, and I thank You for these lessons.

Winter Snow

What a beautiful illustration of purity You've given us in a blanket of fresh-fallen snow. It's the kind of purity You want for my life, and it's the cleanliness that only You can give. I am so grateful for Your saving blood that washed my life white as snow.

Cleansing Flames

You wanted to use me, Father, but You knew there were areas in my heart that first needed cleansing. You knew the only way to accomplish this would be to send purifying flames. The testing fires were painful sometimes, but I'm glad You sent them. It felt good to be washed and worthy of service.

_____

_____

_____

_____

_____

_____

_____

_____

_____

_____

_____

_____

_____

_____

_____

_____

_____

_____

_____

_____

_____

_____

_____

_____

_____

_____

_____

_____

True Purity

Father, please show me if the life I live is truly pure in Your sight. In my pride, I'm afraid I raise myself to greater heights than I ought to where cleanliness is involved. But I want to see myself through Your eyes. I want to measure up to Your standards. Please purify my attitude, Lord.

Cleanse My Lips

You had a job for Moses, but he said he couldn't speak. Isaiah, on the other hand, was willing. You simply had to cleanse his lips so that the words You gave him would come forth purely. You've given me a message to share, too. I just pray that You would touch my mouth with Your coals.

Relationships

The best relationship is the one in which your love
for each other exceeds your need for each other.

UNKNOWN

People in My Life

I know that You've brought people into my life for many different reasons, but I have to admit
that sometimes I'd like to take my dog and move to my own island. It's hard to please people, and
it's easy to upset them. Neither situation is pleasant for me. Lord, please help me do my best in
each relationship.

The Best Relationship

Dear Jesus, I've known many people in my life. I've enjoyed many good relationships and tried to avoid the bad. One thing is certain, though. My relationship with You is the most important. I'm so glad You have time for me and that You want me to fellowship with You. I couldn't ask for a better friend.

_____

_____

_____

_____

_____

_____

_____

_____

_____

_____

_____

_____

_____

_____

_____

_____

_____

_____

_____

_____

Harmful Relationships

Lord, I generally think of relationships as being between people, and I fail to remember that my relationship to things can seriously affect how I react to people. For instance, sometimes I get so involved in a television show that I fail to give needed attention to my family. Forgive me, Father. Be in charge of my relationships.

Good Relationships

Thank You, Lord, for giving me a good relationship with my husband and children. So many people struggle with unhappy homes, and it's only Your grace that protects me from that. I ask that You'd keep Your hand on our home and give others happy lives, as well.

_____

_____

_____

_____

_____

_____

_____

_____

_____

_____

_____

_____

_____

_____

_____

_____

_____

Expert Advice

I am amazed at the wisdom that King Solomon extended to his son in the Proverbs, Lord. I guess
he would have had expert knowledge concerning relationships, though, since he'd been involved
in so many. I'm glad he talks about both the good and the bad, too. It gives me courage to choose
good companions.

Rest

Rest is not idleness, and to lie sometimes on the grass under the trees on a summer's day, listening to the murmur of water, or watching the clouds float across the sky, is by no means a waste of time.

JOHN LUBBOCK

Finding Time to Rest

I find it difficult to even sit down to a meal, Father. Resting seems like such a far-fetched notion. I know You want me to find time to rest and spend time with You, but I'm on the go constantly, and I still don't get everything done. Please help me, Lord, to make resting a priority.

_____

_____

_____

_____

_____

_____

_____

_____

_____

_____

_____

_____

_____

_____

_____

_____

Resting on the Porch Swing

In my mind, resting usually translates into sleep, but as I sit here on the porch swing, gliding slowly back and forth, and thinking about nothing in particular, I am reminded that relaxing takes on many forms. I feel blessed indeed that rest is part of Your plan.

Balancing Work and Rest

I had to chuckle as I read the verse that says, "Give not sleep to thine eyes" (Proverbs 6:4). I guess I don't have much trouble obeying that! I have more difficulty with "Come. . .apart. . .and rest a while" (Mark 6:31). I think I'm getting the picture, though. Please help me learn to balance work and rest.

_____

_____

_____

_____

_____

_____

_____

_____

_____

_____

_____

_____

_____

_____

_____

_____

_____

_____

_____

_____

_____

_____

_____

_____

_____

_____

_____

_____

_____

_____

_____

_____

_____

A Day of Rest

You established a day of rest following Your completion of creation, God. Although You expect us to spend time with You daily, You knew how much we would need a day to retreat from our normal activities, to fellowship with other believers, and to focus primarily on You. Help me never take this day of rest for granted.

Entering God's Rest

Dear Jesus, in this world, we will never experience true rest, but You've offered this tantalizing refreshment to anyone who will enter it. Yet so many reject this repose You offer. It's a refusal I can't fathom, Lord. Show them what they are missing. Draw them into Your rest today.

_____

_____

_____

_____

_____

_____

_____

_____

_____

_____

_____

_____

_____

_____

_____

_____

_____

_____

_____

_____

_____

_____

_____

_____

_____

_____

Salvation

No man can fail of the benefits of Christ's salvation,
but through an unwillingness to have it.

WILLIAM LAW

The Greatest Salvation

Salvation is something we all long for in one way or another, Father, and the salvation You've provided far surpasses anything that could be presented by mankind. You've rescued me from the depths of sin and given me new life in Christ, and I will ever praise You!

Salvation of Loved Ones

There are many people in my family who have not accepted Your gift of salvation, dear Jesus. My most heartfelt prayer for each of them is that they will trust You. Draw each of them into Your embrace. I pray that each would receive You as Savior.

_____

_____

_____

_____

_____

_____

_____

_____

_____

_____

_____

_____

_____

_____

_____

_____

_____

_____

_____

_____

_____

_____

_____

_____

_____

_____

_____

_____

_____

_____

Let the Children Come

You said that accepting You requires childlike faith, dear Jesus. Yet so often we fail to take the young ones seriously. We think they're too young to understand, but You said to let them come. Give us wisdom when dealing with the little ones, and help us encourage them to accept You, as well.

Stand Still, and See

the Salvation of the Lord

We are such a frenetic lot, dear God, but when we get all worked up, You say, "Stand still." You offer complete salvation but only when we take the time to see from where our deliverance comes. Help us slow down and witness the greatest of miracles.

_____

_____

_____

_____

_____

_____

_____

_____

_____

_____

_____

_____

_____

_____

_____

_____

Good Enough?

When I stand before the Great White Throne, won't it be enough that I was a good person? Won't it matter that I went to church and tithed? I even taught Sunday school. Will You really say, "Depart from me" (Matthew 25:41)? Is that what Your Word means by, "Not by works of righteousness. . .but according to his mercy he saved us" (Titus 3:5)?

Self-Esteem

Christlikeness

There's such a fine line between self-esteem and arrogance. Sometimes I have trouble distinguishing between the two. Father, You created me in Your image. For that I am thankful, but I need to remember that I'm not perfect. Help me not to be proud but to daily strive to be more like You.

_____

_____

_____

_____

_____

_____

_____

_____

_____

_____

_____

_____

_____

_____

_____

_____

_____

_____

_____

_____

_____

_____

_____

_____

_____

_____

Building Self-Esteem

I remember when I was little how embarrassing it was to be teased about my nerdy assortment of clothing. And it hurt when the "big kids" picked on me, but You also brought people into my life who uplifted and encouraged me. What a blessing they were! Lord, let me build another person's self-esteem.

Affecting Others

Lately I've been feeling a little low, Father. I'm not meeting those expectations I have of myself, and I've been dragging myself down. Unfortunately, my lack of self-esteem is pulling others down, too. I don't want to do that. I want to give my frustrations to You and let You work through me.

_____

_____

_____

_____

_____

_____

_____

_____

_____

_____

_____

_____

_____

_____

Special to the Father

How can I doubt my worth in Your eyes, Father? You know the number of hairs on my head. You created me, and You said that Your creation is very good. When I'm tempted to get down on myself, remind me that I am special to You, and there's no one just like me.

Still Working on Me

Dear God, I'm a far cry from perfect, but I'm confident in the knowledge that You love me just as I am. You are the One who has begun a work in me, and You will be faithful to complete what has been started. What a thrill to know that You'll make me what You want me to be.

_____

_____

_____

_____

_____

_____

_____

_____

_____

_____

_____

_____

_____

_____

_____

_____

_____

_____

_____

_____

_____

_____

_____

_____

_____

_____

Service

It is distinctive of the Christian life, that while it grows more conscientious,
it also grows less and less a task of duty and more and more a service of delight.

NEWMAN SMYTH

Lessons from Feet

Jesus, I read the story about how You washed Your disciples' feet, and I thought about how unpleasant that might have been. Were You thinking that those same feet would carry Your gospel to the world? They were no longer appalling, but beautiful. I will wash feet if You call me to, or I'll carry Your message.

Saved to Serve

I'm not sure how many times I've heard the saying "God saved me to serve, not to sit." There are so many ways I can be involved in Christian service. What I need most is a willing heart. Help me never to lose sight of the fact that servanthood is beautiful in Your sight and a blessing to others.

_____

_____

_____

_____

_____

_____

_____

_____

_____

_____

_____

_____

_____

It's All Important

You know, when I was little, I had chores to do. I didn't want to do them because they didn't seem important. I wanted to do meaningful work. Now I find myself with the same attitude at times. You show me a job that needs to be done, but I ignore it because I want something more challenging. Forgive me, Lord. In Your eyes it's all important.

A Servant's Heart

The irony in Your Word makes me smile, Lord. When You speak of greatness, it's in connection with servanthood. It's so contrary to human nature, but when I think about it, it really does make sense. That still doesn't make it easy, though. Please give me a servant's heart.

_____

_____

_____

_____

_____

_____

_____

_____

_____

_____

_____

_____

_____

_____

_____

_____

_____

_____

_____

_____

_____

_____

_____

_____

_____

_____

_____

_____

_____

_____

_____

_____

_____

Martha's Trap

Lord, I want to be a servant, but I want it to be done Your way. Please don't let me get caught in Martha's trap of meeting only the physical needs. Although those elements are important, they don't reach the whole person. Let me be a blessing in the spiritual and emotional areas, too.

Stress

The little troubles and worries of life may be as stumbling blocks in our way,
or we may make them stepping-stones to a nobler character and to heaven.

HENRY WARD BEECHER

The Popularity of Stress

Stress seems so overrated these days, doesn't it, Lord? Every time I turn around, someone is telling me how stressed they are. And I do the same thing. I guess it's popular to be stressed. Popular maybe—but not good. Please take my stress and turn it into energy that is used for Your glory.

_____

_____

_____

_____

_____

_____

_____

_____

_____

_____

_____

_____

_____

_____

_____

_____

_____

_____

_____

_____

_____

_____

_____

_____

_____

_____

_____

_____

_____

A Load of Stress

Deadlines, sports schedules, unexpected overnight company—I'm about to pull out my hair!
I know we all have our share of stress, but didn't I get an extra load this week, Father? I'm not sure
what the purpose of it is, but I know there's a reason. Lord, give me patience through the ordeal,
and let me please You.

One Step at a Time

It's the end of another day, Father. I didn't accomplish enough, and tomorrow looms nearby with all of its expectations. I want to rejoice in the days You give me, but honestly it's been a chore merely to put one foot in front of the other. The stress of the load weighs me down. Please grant me the strength to take one step at a time.

_____

_____

_____

_____

_____

_____

_____

_____

_____

_____

_____

_____

_____

_____

_____

_____

_____

_____

_____

_____

_____

_____

_____

_____

_____

_____

_____

_____

_____

_____

_____

_____

_____

Stress and Vulnerability

Dear God, I've discovered that during these times of stress I seem more vulnerable to temptation. I need You even more during this trying hour. I must lean on You and on the godly friends You've provided. Help me to focus on the goal, and keep me from faltering.

I Failed to Trust You

Forgive me, Father. Time and again I've been so stressed that I wanted to give up on life. I tried so hard to get through each day, but I never bothered to give my worries to You. I've fought through each task and brought grief to others by trying to struggle alone, but from now on, I'm casting my cares on You!

_____

_____

_____

_____

_____

_____

_____

_____

_____

_____

_____

_____

_____

_____

_____

_____

_____

_____

_____

_____

_____

_____

_____

_____

_____

_____

True Beauty

Favour is deceitful, and beauty is vain: but a woman
that feareth the LORD, she shall be praised.

PROVERBS 31:30

Lessons from a Child

I saw the prettiest child at the park today, Father. Her beautiful smile reached her eyes. I think it must have reached her heart, too, because I also saw this little girl go right up and play with a child who had a disability, and whom other kids were teasing. Lord, thank You for showing me what inner beauty is.

The Beauty of Christ

You know, Lord, I spend a lot of time each morning trying to look physically attractive. That doesn't do much for my soul, though. Sure, I feel better when I look nice, but I know if people saw Your beauty in me, that would bring more joy. Draw me close, and make this a reality.

_____

_____

_____

_____

_____

_____

_____

_____

_____

_____

_____

_____

_____

_____

_____

In Spite of the Grime

This afternoon I asked my husband to help me with a task that was neither clean nor fun. When we'd completed the chore, we were both filthy. But at that moment I saw a beautiful person. He had other plans, but because I needed help, he gave willingly. That's beautiful!

Incorruptible Beauty

I was glancing through a magazine today, and there were so many tips on being beautiful. As I looked at the models, I thought about how few people really look like that. And I realized something like a car crash could change it all instantly. Inner beauty isn't like that, is it, Father? It's from You, and it's incorruptible.

_____

_____

_____

_____

_____

_____

_____

_____

_____

_____

_____

_____

_____

_____

_____

Already Beautiful

Yesterday I heard a little boy ask his mother why she was purchasing cosmetics. "To help me look better," was her reply. "But you're beautiful," the boy said with conviction. The mother smiled brightly and gave the child a hug. As he returned the embrace, the love between them was unmistakable. Lord, at that moment I knew—she was beautiful!

Wisdom

Pure wisdom always directs itself toward God;
the purest wisdom is knowledge of God.

LEW WALLACE

God's Wisdom

I'm so forgetful! God, I know how many times You've admonished me to seek Your wisdom, yet over and over I try to do things on my own. You'd think I would learn after so many mistakes, but I guess I'm too proud. I don't want to continue like this. I want Your wisdom so that I can live life as You intended.

_____

_____

_____

_____

_____

_____

_____

_____

_____

_____

_____

_____

_____

_____

_____

_____

_____

_____

_____

_____

_____

_____

_____

_____

_____

_____

_____

_____

_____

_____

Making Decisions

I'm facing a situation right now, and I'm not quite sure how to handle it, Father. I'm coming to You because I truly lack wisdom, but I need to know how to make the right decision. Thank You for promising that You will guide me.

God's Book of Wisdom

There are so many "how-to" books available today, Lord, and they all promise to increase my knowledge in some area. But not one of them gives any hope for added wisdom. Only Your Word offers that. Thank You for providing the means to know You more fully and to live life more abundantly.

_____

_____

_____

_____

_____

_____

_____

_____

_____

_____

_____

_____

_____

_____

_____

_____

_____

Solomon's Choice

You gave Solomon an opportunity to ask of You any gift he desired, and he asked for wisdom.
Thus he received many more blessings. I'd like to think I would have asked the same, but I don't
know if I would have. Please make me more mature so I'll ask for things that really matter.

Having Wisdom and Applying It

Lord, You've given me a wealth of wisdom right there in Your Word, but knowing what's there and acting upon it are two entirely different things. Sometimes my behavior is still so foolish. Forgive me, Lord. Help me not to ignore the direction You've given me. Help me to walk wisely.

_____

_____

_____

_____

_____

_____

_____

_____

_____

_____

_____

_____

_____

_____

Work

Opportunity is missed by most people because
it comes dressed in overalls and looks like work.

THOMAS EDISON

Prioritizing

Father, I really have a lot to do, and I'm not very good at multitasking. I need Your help each day as I organize the chores that need to be done. Show me how to prioritize my workload so that I can get things done in the most efficient manner, and let my work be pleasing in Your sight.

Enjoyable Work

I'm blessed to have a job I enjoy, Lord. So many people aren't able to say the same, and many of them probably have good reason to dislike their work. Thank You for opening this door of opportunity for me. You've met my needs in a wonderful way.

_____

_____

_____

_____

_____

_____

_____

_____

_____

_____

_____

_____

_____

_____

_____

_____

_____

_____

_____

_____

_____

_____

_____

_____

_____

_____

_____

_____

Difficult Coworkers

I don't know how much longer I can take this. Father, when I accepted this job I really thought I was getting into a good situation, but the people I work with are so fake. Everyone is in it for self-gratification—not for the company or those we serve. I'm so tired of it. Please help me through this difficult time.

Workaholic

Is this really healthy, Lord? The more I work, the more I find that needs to be done. It seems I'm only content when I'm busy, but even though accomplishments are exciting, I seem to be missing out on simple pleasures. I really want to learn to enjoy stopping to smell the roses.

_____

_____

_____

_____

_____

_____

_____

_____

_____

_____

_____

_____

_____

_____

_____

_____

_____

_____

_____

_____

_____

_____

_____

_____

_____

_____

_____

_____

_____

_____

_____

Menial Tasks

Do You ever wish we'd eliminate the phrase "menial task" from our vocabulary, Father? I know that all work is important to You and that the attitude I have when performing each duty holds even greater weight. Help me to remember that even the small jobs have significance in light of the bigger picture.

Date: _____

New prayer requests: _____

_____

_____

_____

_____

_____

_____

_____

Ongoing prayer requests: _____

_____

_____

_____

_____

_____

Answers to prayer: _____

_____

_____

_____

_____

_____

_____

_____

_____

_____

Praises: _____

_____

_____

_____

_____

_____

_____

_____

Date: _____

New prayer requests: _____

_____

_____

_____

_____

_____

_____

_____

_____

Ongoing prayer requests: _____

_____

_____

_____

_____

_____

_____

Answers to prayer: _____
_____
_____
_____
_____
_____
_____
_____
_____
_____
_____
_____

Praises: _____
_____
_____
_____
_____
_____
_____
_____
_____

Date: _____

New prayer requests: _____

_____

_____

_____

_____

_____

_____

_____

Ongoing prayer requests: _____

_____

_____

_____

_____

_____

_____

Answers to prayer: _____
_____
_____
_____
_____
_____
_____
_____
_____
_____

Praises: _____
_____
_____
_____
_____
_____
_____
_____
_____

Date: _____

New prayer requests: _____

_____

_____

_____

_____

_____

_____

_____

_____

Ongoing prayer requests: _____

_____

_____

_____

_____

_____

_____

_____

Answers to prayer: _____

_____

_____

_____

_____

_____

_____

_____

_____

_____

_____

_____

Praises: _____

_____

_____

_____

_____

_____

_____

_____

_____

Date: _____

New prayer requests: _____

_____

_____

_____

_____

_____

_____

_____

_____

Ongoing prayer requests: _____

_____

_____

_____

_____

_____

_____

_____

Answers to prayer: _____

_____

_____

_____

_____

_____

_____

_____

_____

_____

Praises: _____

_____

_____

_____

_____

_____

_____

_____

Date: _____

New prayer requests: _____

_____

_____

_____

_____

_____

_____

_____

_____

Ongoing prayer requests: _____

_____

_____

_____

_____

_____

_____

Answers to prayer: _____

_____

_____

_____

_____

_____

_____

_____

_____

_____

Praises: _____

_____

_____

_____

_____

_____

_____

_____

Date: _____

New prayer requests: _____

_____

_____

_____

_____

_____

_____

_____

_____

Ongoing prayer requests: _____

_____

_____

_____

_____

_____

_____

Answers to prayer: _____

_____

_____

_____

_____

_____

_____

_____

_____

_____

_____

Praises: _____

_____

_____

_____

_____

_____

_____

_____

_____

Date: _____

New prayer requests: _____
_____
_____
_____
_____
_____
_____
_____
_____

Ongoing prayer requests: _____
_____
_____
_____
_____
_____
_____
_____

Answers to prayer: _____

_____

_____

_____

_____

_____

_____

_____

_____

_____

Praises: _____

_____

_____

_____

_____

_____

_____

_____